MA1

the faith of a

Mockingbird

LEADER GUIDE
WRITTEN BY JOSH TINLEY

A SMALL GROUP STUDY
CONNECTING CHRIST AND CULTURE

Abingdon Press / Nashville

THE FAITH OF A MOCKINGBIRD
LEADER GUIDE
by Josh Tinley

A SMALL GROUP STUDY
CONNECTING CHRIST AND CULTURE

This book is printed on elemental chlorine-free paper.
ISBN 978-1-5018-0371-0

15 16 17 18 19 20 21 22 23—10 9 8 7 6 5 4 3 2 1
MANUFACTURED IN THE UNITED STATES OF AMERICA

_,50_

CONTENTS

the Faith of a

Mockingbird

TO THE LEADER

This Pop in Culture Bible study series is a collection of studies about faith and popular culture. Each study uses a work of pop culture as a way to examine questions and issues of the Christian faith. Studies consist of a book, DVD, and leader guide. Our hope and prayer is that the studies will open our eyes to the spiritual truths that exist all around us in books, movies, music, and television.

As we walk with Christ, we discover the divine all around us, and in turn, the world invites us into a deeper picture of its Creator. Through this lens of God's redemption story, we are invited to look at culture in a new and inviting way. We are invited to dive into the realms of literature, art, and entertainment to explore and discover how God is working in and through us and in the world around us to tell his great story of redemption.

Sin and redemption and wisdom and love are all themes that comprise Harper Lee's masterpiece, *To Kill a Mockingbird.*

An influential and transformative work, *To Kill a Mockingbird* is one piece of popular culture that has certainly withstood the test of time. In his study *The Faith of a Mockingbird,* author and pastor Matt Rawle takes us on a tour of Harper Lee's classic novel, examining the perspectives and experiences of four key characters and exploring how this novel serves as a lens through which we can understand our place in the world, how we play a role in God's story, and what it means to live out a hopeful faith in a broken world.

In this study, we will explore the attributes and lives of four of the book's main characters—Scout Finch, Atticus Finch, Tom Robinson, and Boo Radley—and what each can teach us about faith and redemption.

HOW TO FACILITATE THIS STUDY

Participants in this study do not need to have read *To Kill a Mockingbird.* That said, your group will likely get more out of this study if participants have some familiarity with the story. It would even be a good idea to get together as a group and watch the film version of the novel before your first session. The study book contains a quick refresher of the book in the introductory material, and has character sketches and plot lines throughout the book so members can familiarize themselves with the key aspects of the novel. It is also important that participants take time before each session to read the corresponding chapter in *The Faith of a Mockingbird* and reflect on its questions.

This four-session study uses the following components:

- the study book, *The Faith of a Mockingbird* by Matt Rawle
- this Leader Guide
- *The Faith of a Mockingbird* DVD

You will need a DVD player or computer, and a television or projection screen so that you can watch the DVD segments as part of your group session. Participants in the study will also need access to Bibles during the session; many activities will also require basic supplies including a markerboard or large sheets of paper and markers, pens and pencils, and index cards and/or slips of paper.

Each session is structured into a 60-minute format:

- Opening Activity and Prayer (5 minutes)
- Watch DVD Segment (10 minutes)
- Study and Discussion (35 minutes)
- Closing Activity and Prayer (10 minutes)

If you have more time in your session, or want to utilize more activities during your session, "Additional Options for Bible Study and Discussion" are included for each chapter, listed after the closing prayer.

Helpful Hints

Preparing for Each Session

- Pray for wisdom and discernment from the Holy Spirit, for you and for each member of the group, as you prepare for the study.

- Before each session, familiarize yourself with the content. Read the study book chapter again.
- Choose the session elements you will use during the group session, including the specific discussion questions you plan to cover. Be prepared, however, to adjust the session as group members interact and as questions arise. Prepare carefully, but allow space for the Holy Spirit to move in and through the group members and through you as facilitator.
- Prepare the space where the group will meet so that the space will enhance the learning process. Ideally, group members should be seated around a table or in a circle so that all can see one another. Moveable chairs are best, so that the group easily can form pairs or small groups for discussion.

Shaping the Learning Environment

- Create a climate of openness, encouraging group members to participate as they feel comfortable.
- Remember that some people will jump right in with answers and comments, while others need time to process what is being discussed.
- If you notice that some group members seem never to be able to enter the conversation, ask them if they have thoughts to share. Give everyone a chance to talk, but keep the conversation moving. Moderate to prevent a few individuals from doing all the talking.
- Communicate the importance of group discussions and group exercises.
- If no one answers at first during discussions, do not be afraid of silence. Count silently to ten, then say

something such as, "Would anyone like to go first?" If no one responds, venture an answer yourself and ask for comments.

- Model openness as you share with the group. Group members will follow your example. If you limit your sharing to a surface level, others will follow suit.
- Encourage multiple responses before moving on.
- Ask, "Why?" or "Why do you believe that?" or "Can you say more about that?" to help continue a discussion and give it greater depth.
- Affirm others' responses with comments such as "Great" or "Thanks" or "Good insight"—especially if it's the first time someone has spoken during the group session.
- Monitor your own contributions. If you are doing most of the talking, back off so that you do not train the group to listen rather than speak up.
- Remember that you do not have all the answers. Your job is to keep the discussion going and encourage participation.

Managing the Session

- Honor the time schedule. If a session is running longer than expected, get consensus from the group before continuing beyond the agreed-upon ending time.
- Involve group members in various aspects of the group session, such as saying prayers or reading the Scripture.
- Note that the session guides sometimes call for breaking into smaller groups or pairs. This gives everyone a chance to speak and participate fully. Mix up the groups; don't let the same people pair up for every activity.

- As always in discussions that may involve personal sharing, confidentiality is essential. Group members should never pass along stories that have been shared in the group. Remind the group members at each session: confidentiality is crucial to the success of this study.

Session 1

SCOUT FINCH
TELLING YOUR STORY

PLANNING THE SESSION

Session Goals

Through this session's discussion and activities, participants will be encouraged to:

- consider their faith story and how they tell it;
- evaluate the roles they play and the roles they assign to others, and look at how these roles can be limiting or empowering;
- look at how they can grow in relationship with God by developing holy habits;

11

- examine what they can learn by reading and hearing stories—including those in Scripture—from different points of view.

Preparation

- Read and reflect on the first chapter of Matt Rawle's *The Faith of a Mockingbird*.
- Read through this Leader Guide session in its entirety to familiarize yourself with the material being covered.
- Read and reflect on the following Scriptures:
  - ❏ 1 Corinthians 12:4–27
  - ❏ Mark 5:21–43
  - ❏ Luke 7:36–50
  - ❏ Acts 2:42–47
  - ❏ Galatians 5:2–23
  - ❏ 1 Thessalonians 5:17–24
  - ❏ James 5:13–18
- Make sure that you have a markerboard or large sheet of paper on which you can record group members' ideas.
- Have a Bible, paper for taking notes, and a pen or pencil available for every participant.

Opening Activity and Prayer (5 minutes)

As participants arrive, welcome them to this study. Since the subject of this study is Harper Lee's classic novel *To Kill a Mockingbird*, open your time together with a discussion of your experiences with this story. Discuss some of the following questions:

- When did you first encounter this story, and what about this story has stuck with you the most?
- Why do you think Matt Rawle chose this novel? What does this story have to teach Christians?

Lord, as we begin this study, we thank you for the witness of storytellers. We thank you for the story of To Kill a Mockingbird, *for the ways it teaches us and challenges us, and for the questions that it raises. As we reflect on this story, may we also be mindful of your story and how we fit into it. Bless our time together that we can learn from Scripture, from story, and from one another. Amen.*

WATCH DVD SEGMENT
(10 MINUTES)

STUDY AND DISCUSSION
(35 MINUTES)

<u>Note</u>: Discussion helps and questions that correspond to Chapter One: "Scout Finch, Telling Your Story" are provided below. If you have more time in your session, or want to include additional discussion and activities to your time, see "Additional Options for Bible Study and Discussion" at the end of this section, listed after the Closing Activity and Prayer.

Scout's Story

(See *The Faith of a Mockingbird,* pages 20–22)

Read aloud or summarize for the group:

Rawle begins his study of *To Kill a Mockingbird* by looking at the book as the story of its narrator, Scout, and discussing how brokenness frames her story. He notes that the novel opens with Scout saying that her brother Jem broke his arm when he was nearly thirteen. It then takes her the entire book to explain how this event comes to pass. Throughout the novel, Scout is forced to confront brokenness, whether in the form of fear, social injustice, or struggles about identity and belonging. This brokenness shapes her and has a lasting impact on her life.

In his look at brokenness, Rawle tells the story of a woman in his congregation who had grown hopeless because her body was in constant pain. During the sacrament of Holy Communion she experienced an epiphany. "When you broke the bread at the table," she told Rawle, "I realized for the first time in my life that salvation is offered through a broken body, not one that is whole. Though my health is failing, my hope has been restored." This idea of restoration through brokenness is essential to the Christian story.

For discussion:

- How has brokenness shaped your life? What events that were painful at the time have had a lasting impact and have influenced who you are—specifically who you are as a child of God and a follower of Christ?
- Often the brokenness we experience is of our own doing; it is the result of our sin. What have you learned from

pain that you have caused? How have these experiences led to healing or new understandings? Is there healing that still needs to take place?

- Why is brokenness so important to who we are as Christians? How does the fact that "salvation is offered through a broken body" affect how you understand pain and suffering? What does it mean to you that we find wholeness through Jesus' brokenness?
- How do the characters in *To Kill a Mockingbird* learn and grow from the brokenness that surrounds them?
- Is it possible for us to fully experience God's love and grace if we have not first experienced brokenness?
- In what ways are you—and/or your group and congregation—responding to the brokenness you see in your community and world?

Finding Your Place

(See *The Faith of a Mockingbird,* pages 26–29)

Read aloud or summarize for the group:

Scout struggles to find her place in Maycomb. She clashes with her teacher, gets into fights, asks adults tough questions that they don't always want to answer, and often is the odd person out in the games that Jem and Dill play. This is difficult for Scout because the Depression-era South in which she lives is a place where people know their place. As Rawle writes, "Little girls are to wear dresses and remain quiet. Little boys are to mind their fathers and stay out of trouble. Men go to work. Women stay at home, unless they choose to teach or nurse. White folk go here. Black folk stay there. Everyone has her or his neat and predictable place."

For discussion:

- When is knowing your place or role limiting? When is it empowering?
- How do you understand the roles you are playing right now? Who assigned those roles to you?
- Read 1 Corinthians 12:4–11. What role does Scripture assign you?
- In what ways do you (you personally, your group or congregation, or the church in general) limit people by consigning them to a particular role in society? How do we put people in the role of "other" or "outsider"?
- In what ways do you (you personally, your group, or your congregation) help people live into the roles that God is calling and equipping them to play?
- How does your community of faith welcome and invite those on the margins? Who do you need to welcome to your table so that the gospel might come alive for them?

Activity: *Play Your Part*

A major aspect of *To Kill a Mockingbird* is the roles that people play and the places people fit into (or don't fit into). Most of us struggle with questions about the roles we play and how we fit in. Fortunately the Bible addresses this topic and offers some wisdom. In 1 Corinthians 12:12–27, the Apostle Paul likens the church to a human body. As the body has many unique parts, each with a unique and important function, so does the church have many unique members, each with a unique and important purpose.

- Draw a large outline of a human body on a markerboard or large piece of paper (stick figures are just fine!).
- As a group, read 1 Corinthians 12:4–27.
- Ask each group member to consider his or her role in the body of Christ based on this Scripture. What body part would he or she be? (For example, someone who has a gift for seeing needs around them might be the eyes; someone who is ready and able to go anywhere on a moment's notice might be the feet; someone who is skilled as a communicator may be the mouth.) Ask each person to talk about the body part he or she chose and why. Write each person's name next to the corresponding body part on your outline. (If your group is larger than 6–8 people, you may want to divide into smaller groups for this activity.)
- Talk about what it means for each person to be a certain part of the body and how each of them can embrace and grow into those roles.

Making Room for Awe and Wonder
(See *The Faith of a Mockingbird,* pages 34–38)

Read aloud or summarize for the group:

The storyline in *To Kill a Mockingbird* is full of surprises for Scout and her brother Jem. When they attend worship with their caretaker, Calpurnia, at First Purchase African Methodist Episcopal Church, they are surprised to see a congregation that is able to worship without "the usual church affects like an organ, hymnals, and or a bulletin." After Jem is sentenced to read each day to their contrary elderly neighbor Mrs. Dubose, as punishment for destroying her camellia bushes, he and Scout discover that Mrs. Dubose had been struggling to overcome a morphine addiction. Jem's daily reading helped distract her from withdrawal symptoms.

We need surprises in our lives. Interruptions force us to pay attention to people we would otherwise overlook or to see people from new perspectives.

Read Mark 5:21–43. Discuss:

- How was Jesus surprised or interrupted?
- Why do you think the woman who touched Jesus was "full of fear and trembling" when Jesus asked, "Who touched me?" Why do you think Jesus stopped what he was doing to heal the woman who touched him?
- When has an interruption forced you to notice someone you hadn't noticed before or to look at someone in a new way?
- Read Luke 7:36–50, in which a woman, described as a "sinner," anoints Jesus' feet with oil and wipes them with her hair. Who might you dismiss as a "sinner"? How can you better understand and appreciate these persons as people who are also a part of God's story?
- What interruptions in your own life have been life giving? When was the last time God interrupted and surprised you?

CLOSING ACTIVITY AND PRAYER
(10 MINUTES)

Prepare a large sheet of paper by dividing it into four sections. Title one of these sections, "What Christians can learn from Scout Finch." (You will be encouraged to do this activity at the end of each of your sessions, detailing what you've learned about each of the main characters you'll be studying.)

To close your time together, have each person identify one thing he or she has learned about his or her faith by reading and reflecting upon this chapter and Scout's story in *To Kill a Mockingbird*. Have each person write this one thing on the markerboard or sheet of paper under "What Christians can learn from Scout Finch." Invite participants to explain what they added to the list.

Lord, thank you again for the witness of the characters in To Kill a Mockingbird. *Thank you also for the witness of the participants in this group. Empower us as we go from here to live into the roles you have prepared for us. Allow us to be mindful of the experiences and perspectives of everyone we come into contact with so that we will not dismiss them or take them for granted. Guide us as we prepare for the next session. In Jesus' name we pray, amen.*

ADDITIONAL OPTIONS FOR BIBLE STUDY AND DISCUSSION

Four Portraits (20 minutes)
(See *The Faith of a Mockingbird,* pages 23–26)

Read aloud or summarize for the group:

Accounts of the same event can lead us to very different conclusions if these accounts come from different storytellers. As Rawle points out, "If Jem were our *Mockingbird* narrator, the

19

characters would look slightly different," because Jem would likely draw different conclusions about the same events that Scout recounts. Rawle uses this difference in perspectives to look at the four different perspectives on Jesus' life that we find in the New Testament Gospels.

Activity: *Same Story, Four Authors*

The New Testament opens with four accounts of Jesus' life, ministry, death, and resurrection. Scholars typically call the first three Gospels—Matthew, Mark, and Luke—the synoptic gospels because they cover much of the same material. *Synoptic* means "same" or to "see together." Some renderings of parables and miracles in these books are nearly identical, and the common view among New Testament scholars is that Matthew and Luke used Mark as a source and likely used another common source of Jesus' sayings and teachings. Even John's Gospel contains a handful of passages that are similar to those found in the first three.

Despite these similarities, each of the Gospel writers has a unique perspective and makes particular choices about what to include. There are well-known stories that we find only in Matthew (the wise men, the sheep and the goats), Luke (the Christmas story, Jesus' meeting with Zacchaeus), or in John (the wedding at Cana and raising of Lazarus). Each emphasizes different aspects of Jesus' teaching and frames Jesus' story in a different way.

To better appreciate the perspectives of the Gospel writers, look at three events that appear in all four Gospels:

1. Jesus' baptism: Matthew 3:13–17; Mark 1:9–11; Luke 3:21–22; John 1:29–34

2. The feeding of the five thousand: Matthew 14:13–21; Mark 6:32–44; Luke 9:10b–17; John 6:1–15

3. Jesus cleanses the temple: Matthew 21:12–13; Mark 11:15–17; Luke 19:45–46; John 2:14–22 (Notice that John places this story toward the beginning of Jesus' ministry, while the others place it toward the end.)

Pick one of the three events above, and have four people read aloud each of the four Gospel accounts.

Then discuss:

- What are the similarities between these accounts? Which versions are most similar?

- What are the differences between these accounts? Which of the four differs the most from the others?

- What can we learn from hearing stories from different perspectives? Is there a particular portrait of Jesus in the Bible that resonates with you? Why?

- Think about the different choices that each author makes. What do these choices say about what the author wants to emphasize or teach us? How do we benefit from each author's perspective and choices? What would we lose if the Bible contained only one Gospel?

- What keeps us from being able to see things from other points of view?

- Why is it important for us, as Christians, to consider other people's viewpoints? How does seeing different perspectives better enable us to show love and compassion to others?

Wash, Rinse, Repeat (15 minutes)

(See *The Faith of a Mockingbird,* pages 29–34)

Read aloud or summarize for the group:

Scout, in *To Kill a Mockingbird,* has a particular daily routine, structured around daily habits, such as reading each night with her father. Rawle writes, "Scout's life is full of simple habits and habitual honesty. . . . These habits give birth to a habitual honesty in her relationship with Atticus." What is true of Scout and her relationship to her father is also true for us and our relationship with our Heavenly Father.

For discussion:

- What habits are part of your daily routine? How do these habits give your life structure?
- What habits related to your faith have you developed?
- How do your daily habits reveal your faith and values?
- As a group, list on a markerboard or large sheet of paper any spiritual disciplines and practices you can identify. These could include prayer, reading and studying Scripture, worship, Holy Communion, acts of service and justice, and so on. Ask: How do these practices bring you closer to God? Which of these disciplines do you already practice? Which have become daily or weekly habits?
- What is most challenging about turning a spiritual practice into a spiritual habit?
- Read the following Scriptures: Acts 2:42–47; Galatians 5:22–23; 1 Thessalonians 5:17–24; James 5:13–18. What do they say about spiritual practices and habits?

22

Activity:

Give each person a note card. Each person should choose one spiritual practice that he or she can commit to until it becomes a habit. On his or her card, each participant should:

- name the spiritual discipline he or she is committing to,
- set a goal for how frequently he or she will practice this discipline, and
- determine when and where he or she will observe this practice.

Encourage participants to keep this card with them and to place it where it will remind them of their commitment.

the Faith of a

Mockingbird

Session 2

ATTICUS FINCH
WHEN YOUR STORY IS CHALLENGED

PLANNING THE SESSION

Session Goals

Through this session's discussion and activities, participants will be encouraged to:

- discuss what it means to live as a saint, doing all things for God's glory;
- look at what it means for us, as Christians, to strive for perfection;
- examine the power that our words have and how our words influence others;
- look at how we can take a stand for what is good and right and just;
- consider faithful ways to respond to adversity.

Preparation

- Read and reflect on the second chapter of Matt Rawle's *The Faith of a Mockingbird*.
- Read through this Leader's Guide session in its entirety to familiarize yourself with the material being covered.
- Read and reflect on the following Scriptures:
  - ❏ Matthew 5:33–37
  - ❏ Matthew 5:48
  - ❏ Luke 22:47–53
  - ❏ Colossians 3:12–17
- Make sure that you have a markerboard or large sheet of paper on which you can record group members' ideas.
- Have a Bible for every participant.
- Have paper and colored pencils or markers for the "Meet Atticus Finch" activity.

OPENING ACTIVITY AND PRAYER (5 MINUTES)

As participants arrive, welcome them. When most are present, brainstorm a list of words that would describe Atticus Finch, Scout's father and one of the protagonists of *To Kill a Mockingbird*. Make a list on a markerboard or large sheet of paper. (Even if members of the group have not read the book or seen the movie, they should be able to glean characteristics of Atticus from Chapter 2 of Matt Rawle's book.)

Rawle opens the second chapter of *The Faith of a Mockingbird*, "For anyone who has seen the film version of *To Kill a Mockingbird*, it is difficult to think of Atticus Finch as anyone other than Gregory Peck." Peck won an Oscar for his rendition of the elder Finch. Discuss with the group:

- Imagine that a new movie version of *To Kill a Mockingbird* was in the works. What actor would you cast to play Atticus? How, do you think, would this person embody the qualities we've listed?
- Rawle describes Atticus as "the moral backbone of Maycomb," who is "respected because of his intellect, kindness, and polite resolve." Discuss: Who in your congregation or community might you describe as the "moral backbone"—people who are respected for their wisdom and demeanor?

Lord, as we continue this study, give us wisdom, patience, and humility. Thank you for this group and for this opportunity to come together and reflect on what we, as Christians, can learn from a great work of literature. Bless our time together that we can learn from Scripture, from story, and from one another. Amen.

WATCH DVD SEGMENT
(10 MINUTES)

STUDY AND DISCUSSION
(35 MINUTES)

<u>Note:</u> Discussion helps and questions that correspond to Chapter Two: "Atticus Finch: When Your Story Is Challenged" are provided below. If you have more time in your session, or want to include additional discussion and activities to your time, see "Additional Options for Bible Study and Discussion" at the end of this section, listed after the Closing Activity and Prayer.

Hero versus Saint

(See *The Faith of a Mockingbird,* pages 50–53)

Read aloud or summarize for the group:

Clearly, Atticus Finch stands out as a superhero amidst the many social injustices present in Maycomb County. Matt Rawle calls Atticus Finch "a superhero who fights for truth, justice, and the American Way." He then explains that, "What endears us to superheroes isn't their commitment to the good; rather it is their ability to overcome adversity while maintaining a consistent moral code."

Look at what Rawle has to say on page 41 about how Atticus handles the adversity that comes his way, and his family's way, after he takes Tom Robinson's case: "Atticus represents what it means to fall upward—to lose well. Ultimately Atticus models the Christian ethics of strength through sacrifice and defeat as victory, a way of life rooted in Christ's suffering, death, and resurrection."

For discussion:

- As a group, spend a moment discussing your under-standings of the word *saint*. How do you understand this term? Who would you consider a saint?

Activity:

- Divide into teams of three or four. Have each team read through the characteristics between heroes and saints given in *The Faith of a Mockingbird* (pages 50-51) and identify ways in which a hero differs from a saint. Based on these distinctions, each team should think of a few examples of heroes and a few examples of saints. After a few minutes, have each team name the differences it found and the examples of heroes and saints it gave.

- Different Christian traditions approach the idea of saints differently. The Roman Catholic Church recognizes certain persons as saints, through the process of canonization. These persons are deceased and believed to be in heaven. Protestant Churches take a less formal view of sainthood. Some use the term to refer to those widely considered holy. Some recognize all Christian believers as saints. Some avoid the term altogether. If you'd like, talk about how your denomination and/or congregation understands the saints and sainthood.

- Matt Rawle says that one difference between a saint and a hero is that "the hero's story is about the hero and his or her accomplishments," while the "saint's story is always really a story about God." A saint's story is a story about God because saints do all that they do for God's glory.

Read Colossians 3:12–17 as a group and discuss:

- What does it mean to do all things in God's name and for God's glory? What difference does it make to do things for God's glory rather than for other reasons?
- How can we "put on" traits such as "compassion, kindness, humility, gentleness, and patience"?
- Have members identify something they routinely do each day or week. How could they do this daily or weekly task for God's glory? (For instance, what does it mean to lead a staff meeting for God's glory or to drive a carpool for God's glory? Have participants discuss these questions with a partner, if your group is large.)

Walking Around in Someone Else's Skin

(See *The Faith of a Mockingbird*, pages 57–61)

Activity:

Reread Matt Rawle's account of the mission trip he went on as a ninth grader on pages 58-59 of *The Faith of a Mockingbird*. Then allow everyone time to reflect on a similar experience from his or her own life—a time when he or she came to a greater understanding of someone after seeing things from that person's perspective. If people feel comfortable doing so, invite them to share this experience with the group.

Then have members of the group pair off. One person in each pair should spend exactly one minute describing to his or her partner one important experience from his or her life. The partner should listen closely and, afterward, repeat, as closely as possible, what he or she heard. Partners should repeat this process, this time with the roles reversed. Come back together as a group and discuss:

- How difficult was it for you to listen intently to your partner?
- How closely did you find you were able to retell your partner's story?
- Why is it important that we listen to and learn other people's stories?
- How might your interactions with people change if you took the time and effort to try to see from their perspective?

More Than a Compromise

(See *The Faith of a Mockingbird,* pages 46–50)

Read aloud or summarize for the group:

Rawle writes, "Atticus is the perfect parent, and it nearly makes me sick." Rawle then concedes he's being too hard on himself, leading him into a discussion about perfection and the pressure we often feel to live up to a certain standard.

For discussion:

- In what areas of your life do you feel pressure to live up to a certain ideal?
- Who puts pressure on you to be perfect or to live up to an ideal? To what extent do you put pressure on yourself? Is this pressure you feel a healthy one? Is it effective? Does it bring you closer to perfection?
- Think about the ways you strive for perfection or to reach a certain ideal. How does your standard of perfection differ from what others might want or expect from you? For instance, how might your idea of what makes a perfect parent differ from your children's understanding of perfection?
- Matthew 5:48 says, "Be perfect, therefore, as your heavenly Father is perfect" (NRSV). Other translations say, "Be complete." What does it mean for us to be perfect, or complete, as God is perfect?

Read aloud or summarize for the group:

Rawle recalls a moment in *To Kill a Mockingbird* in which Atticus asks Scout if she knows the meaning of the word *compromise.* Scout has learned how to read (along with several other academic skills) from her father, but her teacher wants Scout to limit her learning to what is covered at school. Scout is upset and decides that she'll quit school. Atticus suggests a compromise: if Scout will go to school, they will continue reading together; Scout just won't tell her teacher about these home reading sessions.

- What are some compromises you've had to make, whether with a family member, coworker, supervisor, friend, or someone else?
- When have you offered a compromise to God? (For example, "God, if you give me this, I promise I'll do . . .") What happened?
- Do you think that God is interested in such compromises? Why, or why not?
- Rawle writes, "The covenant established in the person of Jesus Christ is more than a compromise—it is the solution." What is the difference between a compromise and the covenant that God made with us when he sent Jesus to earth? How is God's covenant better than a compromise?

CLOSING ACTIVITY AND PRAYER
(10 MINUTES)

Refer back to the large sheet of paper you prepared for the previous session. Title the second of the four sections, "What Christians can learn from Atticus Finch." To close your time together, have each person identify one thing he or she has learned about his or her faith by reading and reflecting upon this chapter and Atticus' story in *To Kill a Mockingbird*. Have each person write this one thing on the markerboard or sheet of paper under "What Christians can learn from Atticus Finch." Invite participants to explain what they added to the list.

Lord, thank you again for the witness of the characters in To Kill a Mockingbird. *Thank you also for the witness of the participants in this group. Grant us the wisdom, patience, and courage that we see in the character of Atticus that we might live as saints, doing all things for your glory and not our own. Guide us this week as we strive to do what is good and right and just. In Jesus' name we pray, amen.*

ADDITIONAL OPTIONS FOR BIBLE STUDY AND DISCUSSION

Fighting the Good Fight (15 minutes)
(See *The Faith of a Mockingbird,* pages 54–57)

Read aloud or summarize for the group:

In *To Kill a Mockingbird*, Scout is quick to come to her father's defense, even if doing so means using her fists; but Atticus wants to teach her there are ways to fight that don't involve violence. After establishing this truth, Rawle spends much of the rest of this section discussing how we determine what we should fight for. Most everyone would agree that it is good to take a stand for what is right and just, but how do we know what is right and just?

For discussion:

- What are ways that we, as Christians, can determine what is good and right?
- What resources do we have to guide us when it comes to knowing what is right and just?

Activity:

In *To Kill a Mockingbird,* the decision of whether or not to defend Tom Robinson was an easy one for Atticus. For Scout, on the other hand, the decision her father made wasn't nearly so obvious. As a group, brainstorm some situations or topics for which knowing what is good, right, and just can sometimes be unclear. (This could include a situation as simple as a clerk handing you a $20 bill as change when he was supposed to have handed you a $5; it could also include a hot-button issue such as healthcare or immigration.) Then divide into teams of three or four. Have each team choose one of these situations or topics (or you, as the leader, could assign one to each team). They should then discuss the following questions:

- Why is knowing what is good or right difficult in this situation, or with this topic?
- What do Scripture and the church teach about this issue or topic? How might people interpret this teaching in different ways?
- Where or to whom could you go with questions or concerns about this subject?

The Power of Words (20 minutes)

(See *The Faith of a Mockingbird,* pages 42–46)

Read aloud or summarize for the group:

Atticus Finch is heroic in part because of his wise and effective use of words. His words are as measured when he responds to questions from his children as they are when he presents a case in court. Most of us do not share Atticus' gift for words, so we all can probably identify some situations in which our poor use of words caused unnecessary pain or difficulty.

Atticus relies on his words as a lawyer (though he is aware that winning Tom Robinson's case will be unlikely, no matter how skillfully he pleads his client's case). But he also relies on them as a father. Atticus hopes that he might get Jem and Scout to adulthood without them catching Maycomb's "usual disease" of racism, bitterness, and hate.

For discussion:

- When have you made a regrettable use of words that you wish you could take back? What negative effect did these words have?

- How do your words influence others? How do the things you say affect young people in your care (if applicable), such as children or students? How does being aware of this influence affect what you say, or don't say?

- What responsibility do we have, as Christians, to make wise and faithful use of our words? In what ways do our words, intentionally or unintentionally, reflect on Christ?

Let Your "*Yes*" Mean "Yes"

Toward the end of the section, "The Power of Words," Rawle cites Matthew 5:33–37, Jesus' teaching on the subject of pledges, or oaths. Read these verses as a group. Discuss:

- Why do you think Jesus discourages people from taking oaths or pledges? (This would be the equivalent of swearing by or on someone or something.)
- What are the dangers of swearing when we promise to do something?
- What does it mean to "Let your *yes* mean yes, and your *no* mean no"?

No More of This

Read Luke 22:47–53, an account of Jesus' arrest, in which one of his followers attacks one of the servants of the priest who'd come to arrest him. Compare Jesus' response in these verses to Atticus' response to violence and adversity in *To Kill a Mockingbird*.

- How does Atticus reflect Christ through his words and actions?
- Why is it difficult to respond with love and grace to those who hurt us, even when we know that we should? (Consider how you respond to little conflicts, such as being cut off in traffic or being the target of someone's rude comment.)
- How can we get in the habit of responding to adversity without resorting to violence? (Violence includes not only physical violence but also verbal and psychological violence.)

Session 3

Tom Robinson
When Challenge Is Defining

Planning the Session

Session Goals

Through this session's discussion and activities, participants will be encouraged to:

- consider the role that race plays in their community and world;
- look at factors that divide people into groups and how the gospel can overcome these divides;
- identify examples of injustice in their community;
- discuss how the church can respond to injustice in its midst;
- explore what it means to follow Christ's example of sacrifice when responding to injustice.

Preparation

- Read and reflect on the third chapter of Matt Rawle's *The Faith of a Mockingbird*.
- Read through this Leader Guide session in its entirety to familiarize yourself with the material being covered.
- Read and reflect on the following Scriptures:
  - ❑ Luke 7:36–50
  - ❑ Acts 10
  - ❑ Galatians 3:26–28
  - ❑ Philippians 2:5–11
  - ❑ Colossians 1:15–24
  - ❑ Ephesians 4:11–16
  - ❑ Hebrews 12:1–2
  - ❑ 1 John 4:7–21
- Make sure that you have a markerboard or large sheet of paper on which you can record group members' ideas.
- Have a Bible for every participant.
- If you choose to do the Activity: "Get Sacramental" (on page 47) from the additional options, research your denomination or congregation's understanding of the sacraments, and particularly Holy Communion. Compare your denomination's beliefs about the sacraments to those of other denominations. Some online resources are listed in the activity.

OPENING ACTIVITY AND PRAYER (5 MINUTES)

As participants arrive, welcome them. When most are present, challenge participants to think of an occasion that occurred when they were children or adolescents that seemed horribly unfair at the time. Give everyone a few minutes to think, then invite volunteers to recall these experiences. Ask each person who tells a story:

- Does this experience seem as unfair, in retrospect, as it did at the time? How has your perspective on this experience changed over time?
- What, if anything, is the difference between unfairness and injustice?
- Would you classify any of the stories from earlier as examples of injustice? Why, or why not?
- What comes to mind when you think of injustice? What examples of injustice can you think of?

Lord, as we continue this study, give us wisdom, patience, and humility. Thank you for this group and for this opportunity to come together and reflect on what we, as Christians, can learn from a great work of literature. Bless our time together that we can see and identify ways to respond to injustice in our community and world. Amen.

Watch DVD Segment
(10 Minutes)

Study and Discussion
(35 Minutes)

<u>Note:</u> Discussion helps and questions that correspond to Chapter Three: "Tom Robinson: When Challenge Is Defining" are provided below. If you have more time in your session,

or want to include additional discussion and activities to your time, see "Additional Options for Bible Study and Discussion" at the end of this section, listed after the Closing Activity and Prayer.

Meet Tom Robinson
(See *The Faith of a Mockingbird,* page 64)

Read aloud or summarize for the group:

Tom Robinson is a black man who is wrongly accused, and eventually wrongly convicted, of raping a white woman. While today we may be inclined to say that rape is rape, false accusations are false accusations, and the races of the alleged perpetrator and victim shouldn't matter, race could not be removed from the equation in 1930s Alabama. (And there are still plenty of situations today where race should not be removed from the equation, even if doing so would make us more comfortable.) Rawle writes, "Talking about race can be difficult for many of us."

For discussion:

- Why is talking about race often so difficult? Why do you think it makes us uncomfortable? Race was obviously a major issue back in the 1930s, the time period in which *To Kill a Mockingbird* is set. How much an issue is race today? Specifically, how much of an issue is race in your community today? (If participants disagree, talk about what experiences might be responsible for these differences in perspective.)

- Maycomb, Alabama, is divided along racial lines. To what extent is your community segregated still today?
- What personal experiences have shaped your views of race and racism?
- Based on your knowledge of *To Kill a Mockingbird*, how might Harper Lee's novel—published in 1961 about the author's experiences in the 1930s—inform our conversations about race today?

An Assumed Life

(See *The Faith of a Mockingbird*, pages 66-70)

Activity: *Split-Second Assumptions*

Before the session, prepare sets of one dozen index cards, each with the name of a profession or a role that a person might play. Examples include: "Lawyer," "Custodian," "Stay-at-home Dad," "Police Officer," "Children's Sunday School Teacher," and so on. You should have one set of twelve cards for every two people in your group.

Divide your group into pairs and give each pair a set of cards. Hand them the cards facedown, so that they cannot see what is written on them. Each pair should split the cards so that each person has six cards. On your mark, one person in each pair should show his or her partner his or her top card. As soon as the partner sees what is written on the card, he or she should respond with something he or she might assume about the type of person named. After the pairs go through the first six cards, they should switch roles and go through the other half. (Each person should name six assumptions.)

Note: Use discernment when preparing these cards. If you know there are people in your group who are sensitive about their jobs or about a particular role they play, don't include that occupation or role among your sets of twelve cards.

Discuss:

- Were you hesitant to admit any of your assumptions about these occupations? If so, why?
- Were you surprised by any of your partner's assumptions? If so, why?
- Where do you think these assumptions come from?
- Which of your assumptions are unfair, and how are they unfair?
- What assumptions are at play in *To Kill a Mockingbird*? Which of these are unfair or hurtful? (Draw from your knowledge of the novel or from what Matt Rawle writes in this chapter of *The Faith of a Mockingbird*.)

Read Luke 7:36–50. Discuss:

- What assumptions are at play in this Scripture? How are these assumptions hurtful?
- How does Jesus challenge these assumptions?
- What can we learn from Jesus' teaching in this Scripture? How can we learn from the example of the unnamed woman?

Activity: *Neither Democrat nor Republican*

Much of the conflict in *To Kill a Mockingbird* stems from racial tension. The people of Maycomb make assumptions about one another's character and worth based entirely on skin color.

Galatians 3:26–28 says, "You are all God's children through faith in Christ Jesus. All of you who were baptized into Christ have clothed yourselves with Christ. There is neither Jew nor Greek; there is neither slave nor free, nor is there male and female, for you are all one in Christ Jesus."

- How do the Apostle Paul's words in Galatians 3:26–28 speak to the racial tensions in *To Kill a Mockingbird*? How do they speak to racial conflicts today?

Divide participants into teams of three or four. Have teams add to this verse's "Jew or Gentile" more pairs of groups (for example, white and black, Democrats and Republicans). Give the teams a few minutes to work, and then invite each team to read aloud its expanded version of Galatians 3:26–28.

Discuss:

- How are the pairs of groups you named at odds today?
- How do tensions between these groups affect the church? How can the church work to bridge the divides between these groups?

Fear of the Balcony

(See *The Faith of a Mockingbird,* pages 77–80)

Read aloud or summarize for the group:

In *To Kill a Mockingbird*, Scout, Jem, and Dill arrive late to Tom Robinson's trial, and the only remaining seats are in the designated "colored" balcony. Scout, Jem, and Dill are white, but sitting in the balcony gives them a better view—both literally and figuratively—of all that is going on in the trial. Not only does the balcony view give the kids a better perspective of all that is happening in the courtroom, but sitting there also helps them better understand the perspective of Maycomb's black citizens.

For discussion:

- Ask participants to think of a "balcony experience" from their lives. This could be an occasion when they felt out of place or one when others might have perceived them as being out of place—a situation where they were in the minority because of their race, gender, ethnicity, religion, or other factor. (It's possible that some participants find themselves in such situations every day.) Ask:

  ❏ How were you in the minority in the situation you chose? Did you feel uncomfortable or out of place?

  ❏ What did you learn from this experience, or what are you still learning from this experience? How did this experience give you a new, more complete perspective of your community or world?

  ❏ What might others have learned from you through this experience? Ask participants to think of "balconies" that they may need to visit. Who in their community might they need to spend more time with or get to know better? How can they better know and understand these people without being patronizing?

As time permits, read Acts 10 (the entire chapter). Discuss:

- How was Peter on a "balcony" in this Scripture?
- How did he respond, initially?

- What did Peter learn from this experience? How did this balcony experience better equip Peter to serve God and God's people?

Falling into Hope

(See *The Faith of a Mockingbird,* pages 81–84)

Read aloud or summarize for the group:

To Kill a Mockingbird is ultimately a story of injustice. Tom Robinson, because of his race, is wrongly convicted of a heinous crime. In the end, he's shot and killed in an attempt to escape from prison. The injustice in *Mockingbird* is not only the wrongful conviction but also the social and racial dynamics that prevent a black man from getting a fair trial.

For discussion:

- What is broken in your community?
- What people don't get a fair shake or have limited opportunities to improve their circumstances?
- Martin Luther King, Jr., famously said that injustice anywhere is a threat to justice everywhere. What do you think he meant? What injustices elsewhere are threats to justice in your community?
- How is your congregation working to address injustices in your area?
- Working to deal with injustices often is frustrating and can require sacrifice. But we serve a Lord who was willing to make incredible sacrifices for the cause of justice. Read Philippians 2:5–11 and Colossians 1:15–24.

What do these verses say about the issues of injustice and sacrifice?

- How can you follow Christ's example when responding to injustices in your community?

CLOSING ACTIVITY AND PRAYER
(10 MINUTES)

Refer back to the large sheet of paper you prepared for the previous sessions. Title another one of the four sections on this sheet of paper, "What Christians can learn from Tom Robinson."

To close your time together, have each person identify one thing he or she has learned about his or her faith by reading and reflecting upon this chapter and Tom's experiences and trial in *To Kill a Mockingbird*. Have each person write this one thing on the markerboard or sheet of paper under "What Christians can learn from Tom Robinson." Invite participants to explain what they added to the list.

Lord, thank you again for the witness of the characters in To Kill a Mockingbird. Thank you also for the witness of the participants in this group. Grant us the vision to identify injustice in our midst and the courage to respond. May we follow the example you gave us in the person of Jesus, who was willing to make the ultimate sacrifice to right the ultimate wrong. Guide us this week as we work for the cause of justice. In Jesus' name we pray, amen.

Additional Options for
Bible Study and Discussion

Discussion: *Love and Fear*
(10 minutes)

This chapter in *The Faith of a Mockingbird* examines racial tension and injustice. Discuss:

- How is fear related to prejudice and injustice?
- How does fear divide people?
- What fears might cause someone to be prejudiced toward a group of people?
- How might fear be responsible for division and prejudice in your community and nation?

Read 1 John 4:7–21, emphasizing verse 18. Ask:

- According to these verses, what is the relationship between love and fear?
- How do these verses describe love? Why is there no room for fear in the love that John describes?
- How can the love described in these verses overcome fear?

Activity: *Get Sacramental*
(10 minutes)

To Kill a Mockingbird gives us a feel for the tension between different Protestant groups—particularly Methodists and Baptists—that existed in the Depression-era South. Historically, much of the tension between Christian groups has involved views about the sacraments of baptism and Holy Communion. Rawle writes, "It is a bit ironic that the sacraments, or gifts, God offered to the church in order to bring people together are some of the strongest reasons churches have torn each other apart. Every denomination has its own understanding of what happens at baptism, how Christ is present at Holy Communion, and who is welcome to participate."

Look at your denomination or congregation's official stance on the sacraments of baptism and Holy Communion. Consider the following:

- Who is able to officiate each sacrament?
- Who is eligible to receive each sacrament?
- In what way is God present in each sacrament?

Compare your tradition's view of the sacraments to that of other Christian traditions. There are a host of resources on the Internet you can look to, including:

- United Methodist:
  http://www.umc.org/what-we-believe/sacraments
- Presbyterian Church (USA):
  http://www.presbyterianmission.org/ministries/today/sacraments/
- Episcopal Church:
  http://www.episcopalchurch.org/page/sacraments

Discuss:

- What aspects of the sacrament of Holy Communion are common to all or most Christians?
- Why does our understanding of Holy Communion matter?

- Why does Rawle bring up Holy Communion in the section of this chapter that addresses erasing distinctions based on skin color and other factors?

The Choir and the Jury

(See *The Faith of a Mockingbird*, pages 74–77) *(10 minutes)*

Read aloud or summarize for the group:

At the heart of *To Kill a Mockingbird* is Tom Robinson's trial. Tom ultimately is at the mercy of a jury. Rawle compares the jury in the Robinson trial with the choir at First Purchase African Methodist Episcopal Church, which impresses Scout despite the fact that its singers don't have the luxury of hymnals or songbooks.

Ask anyone in your group who has been part of a musical ensemble:

- What were, or are, the most important factors in determining the quality of your group's performance?
- How did (or does) your group make sure that everyone plays the same piece of music at the same tempo without one voice or instrument dominating the rest?
- Rawle says that, if God's people are a musical ensemble or choir, the "gospel is the piece of music that we are called to sing together."
- What would happen if Christians stop "singing" the gospel?
- What brings us back together when we miss the mark?
- Think of your community as a choir. Which voices are loudest?

- Who does the "choir" look to for leadership?
- How can you (individually or with your congregation) get the "choir" back on track when the voices aren't coming together?

Read Ephesians 4:11–16 and Hebrews 12:1–2. How do these Scriptures add to the discussion?

Boo Radley
Defining a Mystery

Planning the Session

Session Goals

Through this session's discussion and activities, participants will be encouraged to:

- identify and appreciate the mysteries of our faith;
- tell the story of their faith and reflect on how this story influences their behaviors and habits;
- examine factors hindering our understanding Scripture;
- discuss the limitations of human intelligence and the importance of putting our full trust in God;
- look at the Christian faith as a story of light overcoming darkness.

Preparation

- Read and reflect on the fourth chapter of Matt Rawle's *Faith of a Mockingbird*.
- Read through this Leader Guide session in its entirety to familiarize yourself with the material being covered.
- Read and reflect on the following Scriptures:
  - ❏ Job 38:4–11
  - ❏ Psalm 119:169–76
  - ❏ Proverbs 3:5–6
  - ❏ Acts 17:27–28
  - ❏ 1 Corinthians 2:6–13
  - ❏ 1 John 4:1
- Make sure that you have a markerboard or large sheet of paper on which you can record group members' ideas.
- Have a Bible for every participant.
- Review the words from various English dialects for the "Clearing Hurdles" activities. Adjust the word list as necessary for your group.

OPENING ACTIVITY AND PRAYER (5–10 MINUTES)

As participants arrive, welcome them to this study. When most are present, work as a group to tell a story about a mystery in your community. This should not be an actual mystery but a fictional one that you imagine. Ask for a volunteer to start. This person will begin the story with a single sentence. For example, "Fifty years ago, a mysterious creature emerged from a cave on the outskirts of town." The person to the left of the participant who began the story continues the story by adding another sentence. Keep building the story until everyone has had an opportunity to contribute three or four sentences or until the story reaches a satisfying conclusion. Make sure that the story remains focused on some sort of mystery. As needed, interject with an extra sentence to keep the story on track.

Following the story, ask:

- What mysterious tales involving the area where you live do you know of?
- How do these actual mysteries compare to the story we just made up?
- Why are people drawn to mysteries like these, even when these mysteries don't appear to be based on fact?
- Read 1 Corinthians 2:6–13. How is our Christian faith a mysterious faith?
- Ask participants who are familiar with *To Kill a Mockingbird* to say what they know about the character of Boo Radley. What is mysterious about this character? How are the other characters drawn to this mystery?

Lord, as we continue this study, give us wisdom, patience, and humility. Thank you for this group and for this opportunity to come together and reflect on the mysteries of our faith. Bless our time together that we can better identify and appreciate the mysteries and wonders in our midst. Amen.

WATCH DVD SEGMENT
(10 MINUTES)

STUDY AND DISCUSSION
(30-35 MINUTES)

<u>Note:</u> Discussion helps and questions that correspond to Chapter Four: "Boo Radley, Defining a Mystery" are provided below. If you have more time in your session, or want to include additional discussion and activities to your time, see "Additional Options for Bible Study and Discussion" at the end of this section, listed after the Closing Activity and Prayer.

Who Is Boo Radley?
(See *The Faith of a Mockingbird*, pages 87–90)

Read aloud or summarize for the group:

The question, "Who is Boo Radley?" comes up throughout *To Kill a Mockingbird*. Rawle makes the bold assertion that the question, "Who is Boo Radley?" is not unlike the question, "Who is God?"

Activity:

As a group, brainstorm words and/or names that you might use to describe God and list these on a markerboard or large sheet of paper. Once you have four or five listed, go through the words and names. For each one, discuss:

• How do we know that this word or name describes God (from Scripture, from personal experience, from the witness of other Christians, and so forth)?

Next, brainstorm questions the group has about God. List these on a markerboard or large sheet of paper. Discuss:

- Where can we look for answers to these questions?
- Which of these questions can we not know the answers to?
- In what ways must God remain a mystery?

Rawle writes, "Our faith in God, our trust that God will fulfill his promises, grows with our understanding of God."

Discuss:

- How has your understanding of God changed over time? Would you say that you understand God better now than when you were younger?
- In what ways has your faith matured since you were a child?
- Would you agree that your faith and trust in God has grown with your understanding of God?
- Read Job 38:4–11; Psalm 119:169–76; and Acts 17:27–28. How do these Scriptures add to the discussion?

From Story to Communion

(See *The Faith of a Mockingbird,* pages 91–94)

Read aloud or summarize for the group:

The children in *To Kill a Mockingbird*—Scout, Jem, and Dill—take to playing a game called "Boo Radley," in which they act out what they imagine to be the lives of the Radley family. Playing the game reinforces the ideas that the kids have about the Radleys, and reminds us that the stories we tell reinforce who we are and what we believe.

For discussion:

- What story do we, as Christians, have to tell?
- How do we, as the church, tell this story through worship? How do we tell it in other ways?
- How does telling our story teach us about who we are and how we should live as Christians?
- How has your Christian story influenced your actions, behaviors, and habits?
- Rawle writes, "God is not to remain the protagonist of our bedtime stories." What does he mean by this?
- How does God's story challenge you or make you uncomfortable?

Note: If time permits, do "Activity: Be the Story," under Additional Options for Bible Study and Discussion.

Misunderstood

(See *The Faith of a Mockingbird,* pages 94–99)

Activity:

Give each person a half- or quarter-sheet of paper and have everyone list the numbers 1 to 8. Write on a markerboard or large sheet of paper the following terms from different English dialects:

- bucketing
- cobber
- housecoat
- hydro
- mozzie

- speedo
- takeaways
- throwing shapes

Give participants two minutes total to write down what they think is the meaning of each word. After two minutes, reveal the actual meanings and see who correctly identified the most terms. (Feel free to adjust this list of words as necessary. It's important to note that not all Australians or Canadians speak the same dialect or use the same slang. You might also mix in words and phrases from American regional dialects.)

Answers:

- *bucketing* (Irish): raining heavily
- *cobber* (Australian): friend
- *housecoat* (Canadian): bathrobe
- *hydro* (Canadian): electricity
- *mozzie* (New Zealandish): mosquito
- *speedo* (Australian): a car's speedometer
- *takeaways* (New Zealandish): fast food
- *throwing shapes* (Irish): showing off

For discussion:

- Which of these terms were you already familiar with?
- Which would you have trouble understanding, even if you heard or read them in context?

Read aloud or summarize for the group:

Even people who speak the same language can sometimes struggle to understand one another. How much more challenging is it for us to understand Scripture, which was written thousands of years ago in languages very different from ours and by cultures very different from ours?

Activity:

Matt Rawle identifies four hurdles that we must overcome to understand Scripture. Divide participants into four teams and assign each team one of these four hurdles:

- Scripture was written thousands of years ago.
- Scripture was written in several languages other than our own.
- Scripture was produced by cultures with very different worldviews and lifestyles than our own.
- The words in Scripture point to something deeper than their literal meaning.

Each team should discuss the following questions as they pertain to their hurdle (referring back to the "Misunderstood" section of Chapter Four of *The Faith of a Mockingbird*, pages 94–99, as needed). Give teams about five minutes to read and discuss, then invite each team to present its conclusions.

- What challenge does this hurdle pose?
- How have you struggled to get over this hurdle when reading Scripture?
- What resources could you use to get over this hurdle? Why is it important that we be aware of this hurdle when reading Scripture?

Saving a Life

(See *The Faith of a Mockingbird,* pages 103–106)

Read aloud or summarize for the group:

The climax of *To Kill a Mockingbird* involves an event that happens in the dark but is soon brought to light. And while death clouds the ending of *Mockingbird*, there are also glimpses of light and life.

Option: If participants in your group are familiar with the story of *To Kill a Mockingbird* and have read it recently (or seen the movie), briefly discuss the ending. In what ways is justice served? In what ways does injustice persist? If you were writing the ending, what might you have written differently?

Activity:

Light and darkness are used figuratively nearly as often as they are literally. Divide a markerboard or large sheet of paper into two columns. Label one "light" and the other "dark." Come up with as many examples as possible of things that might be described using light and dark. (For instance: light sometimes represents good, while darkness represents evil; light represents knowledge, while darkness represents ignorance.)

For discussion:

- Light and darkness are at the heart of our faith story. How do you see light and darkness at play in the story of our faith?
- Rawle writes: "The gospel doesn't shield us from the ugliness of the world—the prejudice, the hate, the overbearing systems of the world that make justice a

difficult reality—but the gospel, the grace of Jesus Christ giving us access to the love of God, is truly all we need to dispel the darkness and transform death into life." How does the light of Christ reveal the sin and brokenness in the world? How does your faith put the spotlight on realities that you might otherwise be ignorant of?

• How does the light of Christ heal, or have the potential to heal, the brokenness in the world?

CLOSING ACTIVITY AND PRAYER (5 MINUTES)

Refer back to the large sheet of paper you prepared for the previous sessions. Title one of the four sections on this sheet of paper, "What Christians can learn from Boo Radley." To close your time together, have each person identify one thing he or she has learned about his or her faith by reading and reflecting upon this chapter and Boo Radley's story in *To Kill a Mockingbird*. Have each person write this one thing on the markerboard or sheet of paper under "What Christians can learn from Boo Radley." Invite participants to explain what they added to the list.

Lord, thank you again for the witness of the characters in To Kill a Mockingbird. *Thank you for the time we've had together to explore and appreciate the mysteries of our faith. Give us the wisdom to put our trust in you in all that we do. Watch over us as we go from here, that we can live our lives in your light, ready to respond to the brokenness and injustice it reveals. Thank you again for this group and this study. In Jesus' name we pray, amen.*

ADDITIONAL OPTIONS FOR BIBLE STUDY AND DISCUSSION

Activity: *Be the Story* (20 minutes)

Divide participants into teams of three or four. Each team will have the task of telling the story of God's people—from creation to the present—in 90 seconds. Teams can simply tell the story or act it out, but every member of the team should be involved in the storytelling. Allow teams about five minutes to prepare. Then have each team present its version of the story.

Afterward, discuss:

- What parts of the story were included in every team's version?
- What part of the story that your team didn't include do you wish you had included?
- How do you recall this story in your daily life? How do you retell it?

Grace Upon Grace (10 minutes)
(See *The Faith of a Mockingbird*, pages 99–102)

For discussion:

- First John 4:19 says, "We love because God first loved us." God loves us before we have any idea or understanding of who God is. What is your earliest memory of having some concept of God?
- Do you remember a time before you were aware of God? If so, how did your understanding of things or approach to life change after you gained an awareness of God?

- Read what Rawle writes about "prevenient grace" on page 99. Discuss:
  ❏ What is "prevenient grace"?
  ❏ How, according to Rawle, does the character of Boo Radley represent God's prevenient grace?
  ❏ Looking back on your life, can you identify times when God was present and at work in your life, even though you didn't know it at the time?
- Rawle writes that "even in the midst of disobedience, God is still loving and faithful, knowing what we need and offering it to us." How has God shown you love and grace even when you were disobedient or unfaithful?

Activity: *Your Own Intelligence* (10 minutes)

Our understanding always will be incomplete because we are human. Proverbs 3:5–6 says,

> Trust in the Lord with all your heart;
>   don't rely on your own intelligence.
> Know him in all your paths,
>   and he will keep your ways straight.

Divide participants into teams of three or four. Each team should come up with a situation that would demonstrate a person's behavior if he or she were trusting in God versus if he or she were relying on his or her "own intelligence." For example, if a person were to come into possession of a large sum of money, how might his or her response differ depending on whether he or she relied on human intelligence or trusted in God?

After a few minutes, have each team present its situation and contrasting responses. Discuss:

- How can you determine whether an action is based on your own intelligence or on divine wisdom?
- What are the dangers of relying on our own intelligence?
- What does it mean to "Trust in the Lord with all your heart"? How can you know you're trusting in God and not putting your faith in something or someone else?

CPSIA information can be obtained at www.ICGtesting.com
Printed in the USA
LVOW04s1632100815

449281LV00003B/3/P